When Soon Chul Lee's poetry first came across my desk I was struck with the way this poet makes each word count as he says something of value. I wanted the
readers of the Monterey County Herald to hear this poetic voice and appreciate it as I did.
So far, some 30 of his poems have been included in the weekly poetry column, and praise for his work has been heard in many places where poets gather, including places where is known only by those printed words.
We are blessed in this part of California by the presence of many excellent poets willing to share their work with readers of our newspaper. I count the opportunity of reading Soon Chul Lee's submissions as one of the blessings of my job.

Bonnie Gartshore
Poetry Editor
Monterey County Herald
Monterey, California

The Fifth Wheel

Soon Chul Lee

WHYS WORLD PUBLICATIONS P.G., CA

This book is dedicated to
those who love
nature and poetry

CONTENTS

The Tragedy

Crying alone
Inwardly
Not solitary
But lonely

The Affair

Poetry
Being a mirror
To my soul

Seeing
My own reflection
Through it
Looking into others' hearts

It doesn't leave
Me lonely
But apprehensive -
It holds onto my being

Moonstruck

Sat for hours
On the bench
Quiet thoughts lingering -
A boat, poised,
Paused above the lake

One instant
Was caught:
Immortalized
By the proud moon
Of my mind

Moonlight
Showed the blades
And revealed tiny cocoons
With a sudden glimmer
Of everlasting hope

The Naivete

On the seashore,
While I feed squirrels crumbs
Of bread
To feed kids' eyes,
Seafowls flock
Around us;
All the eyes
Towards my left hand -
Relive the childhood memory
Of a mother
With cotton candy

A Poetaster

Eating poetry
I've been living
With a woodpecker

Watching her build
A nest in the tree
Feeding her young
I went behind the clouds
And rose above them
With a skylark

My empty wings
Fear
Being alone
Helpless
While my poems are
Leaving me

Now,
No sky
No wind
Less me

In Seclusion

Wakening
Or sleeping
Dreaming of
Great accomplishments
Cherished desires
Never to be expelled:
Like nature's perennial
In spring
Isolated dreams
Hidden in the heart
Come to flower
Brightly -
To flee
From temptation
I sought the backyard
Drifting
With fallen leaves
For peace

Poet's Corner:
Westminster Abbey

Wandering
Through the times
And minds
You've been with us
And yourselves

In the valley
Of hours
You've hunted
Words
For the song

Being a shelter
From the storm
You, always there,
Quiet, warm,
And loving

Reminiscing

Doll furniture
Was gone
With childhood playmates

Reflecting
In their eyes
Which were twinkling more
Than stars

Their pallid faces
Are flowing away
On a stream
With fallen leaves

Now I scribble
Their names
On the sands

Illusion

Diving deep
Into the music
Of an empty room
I'm
Hypnotized:
Humility is
At the bottom
With Humoresque
Humming
All alone

Bringing joy
Into our being,
Lured
By illusion
I see tears
Washing away the paint
From your face
In front of the dresser -
You're the very picture
Of love

Off-Beat

A thirsty soul
Reeking of liquor,
Pushing my cares
Aside,
Sitting
And lolling on a divan

Out of the tavern
The generous darkness
was waiting
Releasing me
From a matter
Of prestige

Reeling along,
Returning home
The waning moon
Following me
Like a barmaid
With bushy eyebrows

On a Rainy Day

The flow of soul
With you
Becomes an echo,
Knocking on the window

Those last tears
You showed
Are now flowing down
On the window,
Streaming in my veins

Regrettably
Parting with dry lips
I kiss a red wine
That you loved
More than me

The Rejected Assistant

Tapping on the pine,
The woodpecker works on the nailing -
However, I've already fixed
The cupboard!

A Reverie

At 6 am
The alarm hits
My left sensitive ear
And breaks my sweet dream,
I strike the hated intruder

While taking a shower
With closed eyes
The reverie lingers:
I walk
On a rainy road
With the lady
In the dream

I have been to work
With her,
It was a wonderful day -
I saw the sun
Laughing at my foolishness

Lonesome

The loneliness
In living
Makes friends
Of faded albums

Eyes
And eyes
In the photos
Bring names
To mind

The stars
In the sky
Recall those eyes

Behold
We're singing
Nursery rhymes
Together

Heartbreak

In my tiny den
Like a caged bird
Listening to the chirping
Of insects
I see a candle
Guttering down
Silently

As the light
And the sound fade away
Drop by drop
She oozes away
From my memory -
She just melts me
Like candle burning

The Image

Being immature,
Neither child
Nor adult,
A mysterious figure
In the mirror
Looks for its image
But a bearded child
Is nowhere to be seen:
Being in ecstasies
Over the Moon-light Sonata,
Reaching to maturity
Hidden by a tiny modest shadow

After Words

Talked
And talked
With Philip Morris
And Black Russians

Now, my insides
Just feeling like
The empty glass
Though so calm
Being fresh
For the mind
Being blank

Time tests me
Being charmed
By a woman,
Waiting a new
Beginning again

Like a loon
In anxiety
Dimly

Harmony

A meadow bunting
Low flying
In a cloudless sky
Whispers
With the rye grass
Rippling
In the breeze

Under blue, simple blue
Green, simple green
Bending
In a vast field
Is a swaying violinist
Unassuming
Touching
The right chord

Perpetuity

Walking
Through the brush
At dusk,
Meeting an old long shadow -
Inch by inch
It becomes shorter
And rather indistinct
Like my earliest memories

Being restricted
By time, though
Being unaware
Of passage
Of time,
It pleasantly
Passes
Like heady wine

No, not yet
It isn't dark -
See the new moon
Over there
Appearing
From
Behind
The clouds

The Movies

Life is a piece
Of fiction
Or nonfiction

It is with reality
Like water trickling down
A lady's raincoat,
Like her tears

My co-star and I perform
As if we were
A queen and a king,
Or beggars

I practice living
And act out
Fateful scenarios
On a stage

I meet myself
Or my dreamboat
Here and there
On the silver screens

Love

Anything alive
Is lovely
Breathing
Singing
Dancing
With nature -
Without love
The world
Is an empty well

Inspiration

At one time,
All the colors
Of my mind
Being buried
In the weeds
Of hypocrisy
Ailed me:
While getting acquainted
With mossy rocks
Wood rats,
Or hermit thrushes,
Nature
Inspired me
With love
Of poetry -
Returning to mind
My lost colors

A Magic Picture Book

On the playground
Children are playing
Drawing circles

The circles become
Clocks
Scissors
Keys
Knobs
Trains
Moon
Sunflowers
Teachers' glasses
And mothers' faces

The school playground has already become
A magic picture book

In the place
Where children played
And then deserted

Sparrows are gathering
Chirping, chirping
Studying the drawn pictures

The Wharf

See the wind
Touch a waterfowl

Smell the sea ˙
Through its shells

Hear in the shrill
Of steam whistles;
Sounds of my love

Watch fish bones
Floating - the remains
Of souls long gone

Billows of Colors

Under a mackerel sky
Ships are swept away
By the waves

The colors
Are shaped from pearls
Or scales blown
By the wind

A woman painting
Her face thick
Turns pale
At the sounds
Of waves

Dancing with the waves
Or the winds,
She creates billows
Of colors
On a drawing board
Flapping her hair

Daymare

A smog
Laden sky
Watches

A mirror
Smooth sea
Turns oily

A waterfowl
Is sprawled
On the seashore

The earth is dying
With the bird
By day

After seeing
Things to see
Or not to see,
I'm winging
To a forest
Out of a window

Full Moon Junction

After summer light
Has gone to sleep
Wintery shadows
Peek into the window
Likewise,
They
Insensibly
Vanish like smoke -
And yet,
Feeling the sparkle
of love's elation
I soar to the heights
of happy privation
Looking out at the full moon

Motherhood

Laying myself down
Under trees
Laden with fruit,
Looking up at the sky,
Moon Mother
Looking down at me
With her starlit eyes
And persimmon breasts

On a Mother's Day

Yesternight
You were seen
Wearing silver clothes
And raindrops' necklace
In the daisy garden
Which you liked

You were coming serenely
With a smile on your lips
Crossing over to me
With your arms outstretched
Under a white rainbow
After dark

A snowbird
Flew to me,
Sat on my shoulder
And sang a song -
"Life is in a dream,
Come to your dreams . . ."

The place
Where life is eternal
Where only black and white are
I'll go for good
Yesteryear
To you

The dream

Looked just like a snapshot
From my album
Felt a sparkle of your love -
You still love a flower,
A bird, and me

In a Space

Was orphaned
After learning Rilke's "Poet"
In a space
Not bearing a cross
With no paradise
After tearing a red envelope
With whiter teeth
Than snow

Although dreaming flying
Over the Eiffel Tower
Riding on a raven
The space
Like tracks of an arrow
Was covered with snow

The Reborn

A couple of
Shad-flies smear
The windshield;
I find myself
Suddenly awake
From dozing in my seat

Cloud rack
Floating on the ocean,
Dazzling me
With a radiant beauty
Listening to music
Driving by
Pismo Beach

Instantaneously,
Lost consciousness
And found ourselves
In hospital beds
With smashed shad-fly windshield -
Memories
Like an ephemeral existence

Glad to see again
Sunshine
Trees
And faces,
Even an old spider
On the ceiling

A Certain Type

I won't stop
Typing
With my old Underwood
Typewriter
While the woodpecker
Pecks pines -
We race each other

Solitude

The dark
Binding self
Watches me squint
Toward the stars

Night's glow
Shining in my eyes
Falls on a lady's shadow
In the mirror

Hidden feelings
Certain
She'd come
Between two lights

Back to darkness
Recesses
Of the heart
From Hades returning

Observation

Without garbage;
An empty can
Rolling around
With the fickle wind,
As matrimonial
Flitting
To and fro
Leaving a dismal
- Such is life!

Decamp

At morn
And eve
As awaking
And falling asleep,
Punctually
Eking
A scanty livelihood

Spending a lot of time
Getting ready
To finish the work
Within the time
Clutching a straw
Lavishing affection
On this mortal life

Now let me release
Within earthly sins
And be at peace
With Him
Seeing the lines
Converging
Into the new world

The Trail

The shore -
A snake's trail
Passed by
And yet,
I can find
No trace
Of her
But a silver sail
Flapping
In the breeze
Like her chemise

Birdrock Opera

Birdrock
Covered with guano
Of seagulls
Is a stage
On the ocean

Seals are swaying
Wildly singing
Waving their short necks
On the birdrock
Looking up at the seagulls

Seagulls are dancing
Merrily singing
Over the birdrock
In the winds
Looking down at the seals

Seals
Love seagulls
Envying their wings
Wishing to dance with them
In the air

Seagulls are longing to travel
Into the ocean
But are enjoying themselves
On the waves
Like Neptune

Onlookers -
Sea otters
Seabirds, clouds
Are leaving
At sunset

On a Hill

Houses are connected
To each other
Like train cars

Smoking cigars,
Houses are running
Against flowing clouds

However,
The smoke joins
In the clouds

Who knows
Where the long train
Of match boxes goes

But I just see
Houses breathing
Through their chimneys

Holiday Haunts

Where a hawk at leisure
Floats in solitude
Like a kite in the sky
As I dream
On the ground

Only where I can trace the wind
Looking up at clouds
Or feel my age
Hearing waves
At dusk

A tranquil place
For eternal rest
In Big Sur,
Pfeiffer Beach, resides there
Under a tiny hidden valley

My Raccoon

You always stare me
Up and down
With shiny green eyes
Before vanishing
Into the dark

Years ago
When you were little
I saved you struggling
In a garbage pail
In the rain

Then, a few months ago
I saw you nab a nest
From an oak
In our garden --
Lucky you looked so cute
And innocent
You weren't sent to jail

In the backyard
You sometimes dance
With your family
Singing to the moon;
Between curtains
I steal a glance
At your animated shadows

I quite envy you

On a Wintry Eve

On the window sill
A tabby cat
Drops off
To sleep

Her silhouette
Falls on the blanket
Of the bed
While I peek at her

No longer forlorn
Merely cuddling
With her shadow
Purring

Genesis

A eucalyptus tree
Is a larval bed -

Moths sleeping
In the cocoon
Like babies
In the womb

Scraping out
Its leaves
Like tick, tock
Of the clock

Incubating,
Fledging,
To winging

Their dreams
On gossamer wings
Flying high
In summer sky

Like butterflies
Fluttering
From flower to flower
As men court women

The Wind

The wind
Is naked

Sending clouds
To showers
Shifting sands
To hills
Blowing sails
To harbors

Sometimes,
It sleeps
With a mermaid
On a water bed
Of the ocean
On the sand
Of the beach

It is His
Breathing -
Ever abiding
With us

Self-Contradiction

While seeing myself
In the mirror,
He peeps
Into my heart
And spots
Pretense -
Looks more genuine
Than the real one

Amid two faces
Each holds
Its own nature:
He woos me
To go together,
But I ride the tide
At the surge

Hearing
And feeling him
Through all creation,
Haven't seen myself
In the other mind
Without the mirror

Finding myself out,
Anticipating Him,
Till I close two eyes
With one mind
Under one sky

Compassion

A bud
Blooming
Makes me fall
In love -
In the off season
I can see
My love's beauty
Withering away,
As well.
I'm seized
With great pity
For her

Lasagna Woman

Cooking foods
Such sweet perfume
Calls me home

Setting table
I meet my family:
Spoons and chopsticks

Having dry wine
I fantasize about
Her wine red lips

Reflections

My well
Has its own moon
Which captured my eyes

A constant moon
Ever residing there
Outshines the fickle sun

Whatever I sang
The well would
Repeat after me

Hearing frogs' songs
We creatures matured
Together
In my well

To see them
And to find my young eyes
I fantasize about
Returning to a home
Away from home

Star Gaze

The two stars
Chosen and named
By us
Are still looking down
At the bank
Where we're together
And singing

Poppy
And Sequoia
Looking through her
Like every inch a princess
Look at
My silence
And ask
Covering up her
Whereabouts -
Now,
The branches
Swaying about
In the wind,
Softly

A Sweetheart

The shadow
Of a woman
Falls
On the paper window

When the curtain
Was opened
Only the moonlight
Streamed into the room

Her footprints
Were just covered
With unfeeling fallen leaves
On a moonlit garden

The shadow
Of a man
Fell desolately
Over a couple of crying crickets

Mermaids on Carmel Beach

On sunny days
Mermaids cover
The lower half of their bodies
With the white sugar sand

A myriad of sightseers
Passing by there
Unfortunately
Have never seen
A mermaid

However,
Only those
Who see the sand
As sugar
Can see the mermaids

When waves
Or clouds break
The mermaids
All of a sudden
Hide themselves
In the ocean

Even on windy
Or cloudy days
I dream of
Going to the beach
To see the mermaids

On the sugar hill
Like a fairy tale

Land vs Sea

Following up the scent
Of an ocean
The ocean must be a fish
With her skin
Covered by scales -
Five huge fishes
Being alive
Drinking cold water
While six beasts are prey
Surviving by
Sucking hot blood
Of the barren continents

Flying a Kite

Lines of silver
In my hair
Become a spool
Of thread

Disentangling a knot
Of the spool,
Draw a thread
Of light

Embroidering flowers
In the sky
With a thread
With a light,
Travel the world

The smaller
The kite is
The older
I am

It is too long
To reach the sky,
99 years are too short
To count, on the ground

At Twilight

In golden waves
A pair of
Otters
Play hide-and-seek
With an oyster

In the blinking
Of an eye
The beach becomes empty -
The golden hours flow
Into the ocean

Leaving their footprints
In the sand
Seabirds flying
Into the horizon
Golden dots in the sky

Returning home
Under a half moon
Being drunk
Intoxicated with mystery
Of twilight

The Dance

Below the moon,
Sitting on a mossy rock,
Listening to the wind,
My heart dances
With leaves of grass

Under the pine,
Lying on a lawn,
Looking up at the crescent,
My heart goes behind the clouds
With the heavens covered with stars

Silence reigned
All over!
And yet,
We're dark
In the dance

Portrait of Autumn

A fearful season -
When taking walks
Becomes misunderstood
Demonstrations

Mt. Soyo, an entrance
Where recollection
Of deep, green life
Unwillingly
Reddens with death

An invitation
To confidentially talk
In nature's salon
Where speculation
Still marches on

An autumn witch:
Tiny lights of
Luminescent flowers
Are waving their hands
In farewell

Autumn, a sensuous woman
Disrobing by the stream;
Portrait of an image
Love, of my dream

Tulip Dreams

Rough
And tumble life
Always tugs
At a lady's heels

Evening wind
In her face
Let her brows knit

She tramped
Up and down
All day
Leaving footprints
In a snowed in village

Clearing off snow
On the twigs
Of a nameless tree
She's looking for a bud
Awaiting her own spring
As being barenecked
And barelegged

A Gestation

The winter
Nurtures a land's
Pregnancy

Before the land
Ices out
She gives birth

While piercing
The frozen land
A barley's bud
Thrusts out its tiny hands -
How brave it is!

A door
Springs open
To a new world;
The sound awakens
A hibernating frog

Willy-Nilly

In a graveyard
Of thoughts
Entombed
In different eras
I just play
With a blade
Of grass

Meditating

Perfect emptiness
Frees me
From all of society

I hear
Nothing
But feel the air

The still air empties
Into my mind
Through one of the ears

It purifies within
Teaches me
How to live
Where I am

After meditating
I see an old spider
Meditating at a corner
Of the ceiling

Again,
Being on my knees
With both eyes closed
I hold my breath

Curtains

Clouds
Of smoke
Hover over the roof
Like a chemise

Words
From the bottom
Of the pool pour
Like springlets

Deeds
Reflected within
Encounter the bed
Through a mirror

Love
Flowing from the heart
Governs our lives
Indefatigably

A Letter to the Deer
in Pebble Beach

I've never asked
Where you are from
Since we've never shaken hands

I've never asked
Why you live here
Since I live here, too

I've never asked
What you do here
So as not to
Touch your privacy

Let's run away
To wherever it is
To the edge of the ocean
Or the peak in the sky
Where there is no fence
No gate, but nature

If you go
I'll follow
Without wearing shoes or tie
Riding on a hummingbird

Similitude

The curved lines
Of the fine strand
Connecting in silence
One on one
Is the beauty
Of a shapely lady
Lying
On the sand

The Realm

Just now
Release me
From my realm
Of endless thoughts

Under fallen leaves
Leave me
Naked -
Like an autumn twig

Looking into your eyes
I have talked today
About tomorrow -
Putting joy in my being

Savoring your tongue
I have sipped time
And tide
With your shadow

Nevada Falls

There is no bank
　　but a stream

There is no rain
　　but a rainbow

There is no smile
　　but a wraith

Between heaven and hell

There is no bridge
　　but a river

There is no soil
　　but a way

There is no lover
　　but a song

Recollection

Looking up
At a crystalline sky
I see her
Vivid reflection
In water

Looking down
At waving wheat
Undulating
In the wind
I feel her hair
Brushing my face

All at once
A brace of pheasants
Fluttering up
From a wheat field
Shoos away
My dreamy phantoms

Untitled

All through the night
The moon
Hides
Her pregnancy -
A sunflower

Mirror, Mirror

The mirror
Always makes me
Reminiscent
And reminds me
Of lessons
I've forgotten:
The face
In the mirror
Resembles me
And takes pity
On me -
Whenever being bored
Or in deep solitude
I visit him
To be comforted

Thereon,
Washing away
My past scars
On the mirror
Then
I dream of
Meeting her
Whose smile
I saw
Never forgotten

Valuables

After a shower -
Quicksilver teardrops
On the lotus leaves
Of a pond

Pearls
Hanging on webs
At the edge
Of the eaves

As a fowl preens
Herself
Tiny glass beads
Go all to pieces

The epitome
Of valuables
Is a belle's tears
Of joy

Tender Passion

One midnight
The moon undresses herself
Disrobes a virile tree
Beside a lake

She jumps
Into the water
Sleeps with the tree
In the lake

It ripples
The lake
And myself
Too

Street Flowers

Evening - And
Street lamps bloom
Passers-by walk
With light steps

Flowers of flowers,
Pretty women, come out
Passers-by walk in step
Beneath the street lamps

One,
Two,
Three, they are breathing
In the darkness

The Main Attraction

While words
Stumble
From my tongue
With White Russian
In red whispering
Her wishes
To me

In time,
My thoughts return
And speak
With some warmth
About love
And this life -
She has such ingenuity,
Being coy

Coming Home

Playing
With children
I always
Become a child

Loving them
I learn
How to love myself
And others

Through them
I want to redeem myself
Before they see me
As I am

In them
I see my soul
Coming home,
At peace

They're
My poetry
If I'm really
A poet

The Fifth Wheel

Something treated
As a fifth wheel
Sometimes
Incites myself
To poetry
With my horoscope

Even the Furies
With joy
Are beside me
Tossing about
On my bed
In a dire extremity

Putting my shoulders
To wheels
I hear songs
Of birds being
Wafted on the breeze
From the woods

Echoes of a Laugh

Always wearing Red Wing shoes
And a big belt
With screwdrivers and wrenches:
He was "president"
Of Brady's Construction

Didn't look
Like a businessman,
Didn't try to make money,
But wanted to help others:
He was a friend to the poor

One day, after my telling him
I wanted to buy him wine,
He said, "I love Dom Pérignon . . "
But we never shared it:
Always he and I were busy

Last Thursday, leaving,
He said, "See you soon, Soon,"
But he didn't come back -
Dennis . . . no movie title . . .
You were too young to die

My friend,
You didn't die
Just disappeared
With your lovely plane
Amidst soft, deadly fog

Spiritually you've
Never left
Your wife, Kathleen,
Your daughter, Kelly -
Or Kyle, a small carbon copy Mr. Brady

Had I known
You were a pilot
I would have asked
That you not fly
On such an awful day

I used to love the fog,
But no longer . . .
Since it stole you away
Silently as a morsel,
It has become a thief

I thought only oceans
Sometimes swallowed
Human beings . . .
But fog does, too . . .
Bringing with it infinite grief

I've never read poems
To the public . . . and still have not
For this is no reading
But crying out my grief:
For ever do I hear your laugh
                    - In Memory of Dennis Brady
                        1952-1991

Spring News

A wind blows
The fragrant pollen
Of forsythia
To a butterfly
Over a forgotten tomb

About the Author

Soon Chul Lee, author of The Fifth Wheel, was born in Seoul in 1939 and came to San Francisco in 1973.

After completing his doctorate course in education at the University of San Francisco, he taught at George Washington High School in San Francisco. He now is an instructor at the Defense Language Institute in Monterey.

A member of Hubris, the International Society of Poets and the International P.E.N. Club, he has contributed poems to numerous publications, including Visions, Poetry Shell, Quintet in Concert, Voices of America, the Monterey Herald, the San Francisco Quarterly and the National Library of Poetry.

ERRATA:

In Bonnie Gartshore's comment about the author, "he" should be inserted between "where" and "is" -- in the phrase "including places where is known . . ."

In "The Main Attraction" (page 74):

"In red whispering" involves a large omission. "In red lights/She's whispering" is the correct version.

The lines "Was waiting" -- in "Off-Beat" (page 10) -- and "Of love's elation" and "Of happy privation" -- in "Full Moon Junction" (page 27) -- in this printing lack the author's preferred capitalizing of every lines's first letter.